WHAT'S THE WEATHER LIKE TODAY?

By JBus
Illustrated by Viktoria Khmelnickaya

Library For All Ltd.

What's the Weather Like Today?

First published 2024

Published by Library For All Ltd
Email: info@libraryforall.org
URL: libraryforall.org

Our Yarning logo design by Jason Lee, Bidjipidji Art

Original illustrations by Viktoria Khmelnickaya

What's the Weather Like Today?
JBus
ISBN: 978-1-923143-47-0
SKU04318

WHAT'S THE WEATHER LIKE TODAY?

Today, it is sunny.

I can feel the sun.

Today, it is cloudy.

I can see the clouds.

Today, it is hailing.

I can touch the hail.

Today, it is windy.

I can feel the wind.

Today, it is storming.

I can see the lightning.

Today, it is snowing.

I can touch the snow.

Today, it is raining.

I can feel the rain.

Today, it is raining... a lot!

I can see the street flooding.

Today, I am inside.

I can't go out in this weather.

You can use these questions to talk about this book with your family, friends and teachers.

What did you learn from this book?

Describe this book in one word. Funny? Scary? Colourful? Interesting?

How did this book make you feel when you finished reading it?

What was your favourite part of this book?

download our reader app
getlibraryforall.org

About the author

JBus is a Kabi Kabi woman from Queensland and lives in Brisbane. She enjoys being at the beach with her family, creating art and singing.

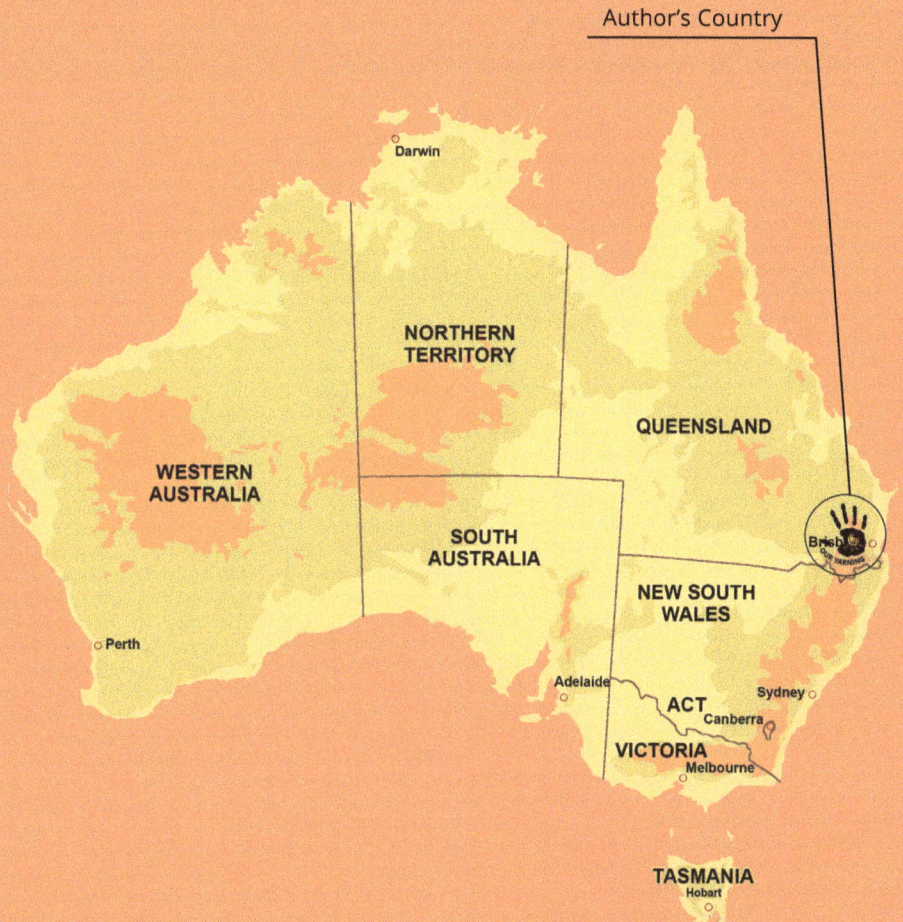

Author's Country

Darwin

NORTHERN
TERRITORY

QUEENSLAND

WESTERN
AUSTRALIA

SOUTH
AUSTRALIA

Brisbane

NEW SOUTH
WALES

Perth

Adelaide

Sydney

ACT
Canberra

VICTORIA

Melbourne

TASMANIA
Hobart

Our Yarning

Want to discover more books from this collection? Our Yarning is a collection of books written by Aboriginal and Torres Strait Islander peoples across Australia.

We know that children learn better, and enjoy reading more, when they see themselves in the stories, characters and illustrations of the books they read.

To download the app, visit the Google Play Store on any Android device and search 'Our Yarning'.

libraryforall.org

www.ingramcontent.com/pod-product-compliance
Lightning Source LLC
Chambersburg PA
CBHW042349040426
42448CB00019B/3469